EMMANUEL JOSEPH

The Art of Alone, How Solitude, Curiosity, and Resilience Shape the Human Spirit

Copyright © 2025 by Emmanuel Joseph

All rights reserved. No part of this publication may be reproduced, stored or transmitted in any form or by any means, electronic, mechanical, photocopying, recording, scanning, or otherwise without written permission from the publisher. It is illegal to copy this book, post it to a website, or distribute it by any other means without permission.

First edition

This book was professionally typeset on Reedsy.
Find out more at reedsy.com

Contents

1. Chapter 1: Introduction to Solitude — 1
2. Chapter 2: The Curious Mind — 3
3. Chapter 3: Resilience in the Face of Adversity — 5
4. Chapter 5: Finding Beauty in the Mundane — 8
5. Chapter 6: The Creative Power of Solitude — 10
6. Chapter 7: Self-Reflection and Personal Growth — 12
7. Chapter 8: The Strength of Vulnerability — 14
8. Chapter 9: Embracing Solitude in Modern Life — 15
9. Chapter 10: The Spiritual Dimensions of Solitude — 17
10. Chapter 11: Solitude and Relationships — 19
11. Chapter 12: The Transformative Power of Silence — 21
12. Chapter 13: Navigating Solitude in Different Life Stages — 23
13. Chapter 14: Solitude as a Source of Innovation — 25
14. Chapter 15: The Role of Nature in Solitude — 27
15. Chapter 16: Community Support for Solitude — 29
16. Chapter 17: Conclusion - The Art of Alone — 31

1

Chapter 1: Introduction to Solitude

Solitude, a state of being alone without feeling lonely, has the potential to unlock one's true essence. In a world that often equates alone time with isolation or sadness, this chapter delves into the profound benefits of solitude. Drawing on personal anecdotes and scientific research, we'll explore how solitude fosters creativity, introspection, and emotional growth. Solitude is not the absence of connection but the presence of self, and learning to embrace it can lead to remarkable revelations about one's desires, motivations, and potential.

Solitude is often misunderstood. Many people view it as a negative state, a sign of loneliness or social failure. However, solitude is a powerful tool for personal growth and self-discovery. In solitude, we find the space to reflect on our lives, our goals, and our values. We can hear our own thoughts without the noise of the outside world. Solitude allows us to connect with our inner selves and understand our true desires and motivations.

Scientific research has shown that solitude can enhance creativity. When we are alone, we have the freedom to think deeply and explore new ideas without the distractions and judgments of others. Many great artists and thinkers, from Virginia Woolf to Vincent van Gogh, have found that solitude is essential for their creative process. In solitude, they can fully immerse themselves in their work and let their imaginations run wild.

Solitude also promotes emotional growth. It gives us the opportunity to process our emotions and develop a deeper understanding of ourselves. In solitude, we can confront our fears, insecurities, and vulnerabilities. We can learn to accept ourselves and develop a sense of self-compassion. This emotional growth makes us more resilient and better equipped to handle the challenges of life.

In conclusion, solitude is not something to be feared or avoided. It is a powerful tool for personal growth, creativity, and emotional resilience. By embracing solitude, we can unlock our true potential and live more fulfilling lives.

2

Chapter 2: The Curious Mind

Curiosity is the engine of self-discovery. When embraced during moments of solitude, curiosity can transform even the most mundane experiences into opportunities for growth and learning. This chapter examines the role of curiosity in shaping the human spirit, highlighting how asking questions and seeking new perspectives leads to a deeper understanding of the world and oneself. Through stories of explorers, scientists, and everyday people, we'll see how a curious mind enriches life and fuels resilience, making solitude not a void to be filled but a canvas for exploration.

Curiosity is more than just a desire to know; it is a driving force that propels us forward in life. In solitude, curiosity becomes a powerful ally, guiding us to explore our inner worlds and the world around us. By asking questions and seeking new perspectives, we can uncover hidden truths and gain a deeper understanding of ourselves.

The stories of great explorers, scientists, and thinkers are often rooted in curiosity. Take, for example, Marie Curie, whose curiosity led her to groundbreaking discoveries in radioactivity. Or consider the everyday person who, through a curious mind, finds joy in learning new skills or exploring new hobbies. Curiosity transforms solitude from a state of being alone into a vibrant journey of discovery.

In solitude, curiosity allows us to see the world through fresh eyes. It encourages us to question the status quo and seek out new experiences. When we embrace our curiosity, we open ourselves up to endless possibilities and opportunities for growth. Solitude becomes a space where we can nurture our inquisitive nature and let our minds wander freely.

Curiosity also fuels resilience. By maintaining a curious mindset, we become more adaptable and open to change. We learn to see challenges as opportunities for growth rather than obstacles. In moments of solitude, curiosity can help us find creative solutions to problems and inspire us to keep moving forward, even in the face of adversity.

In conclusion, curiosity is a powerful force that enriches our lives and fuels personal growth. By embracing curiosity during moments of solitude, we can transform alone time into a canvas for exploration and discovery. Solitude, combined with a curious mind, becomes a wellspring of inspiration and resilience.

3

Chapter 3: Resilience in the Face of Adversity

Resilience is the ability to thrive despite challenges. This chapter explores how solitude can strengthen resilience, providing a sanctuary to process emotions and develop coping strategies. By examining historical figures, such as Nelson Mandela and Frida Kahlo, we'll learn how periods of isolation and solitude can lead to monumental breakthroughs. The solitude experienced during adversity can become a crucible where one's resilience is forged, transforming vulnerability into strength and adversity into opportunity.

Resilience is not just about bouncing back from setbacks; it is about thriving despite them. Solitude plays a crucial role in building resilience, offering a sanctuary where we can process our emotions and develop coping strategies. When faced with adversity, periods of isolation can become transformative experiences that shape our strength and character.

Historical figures like Nelson Mandela and Frida Kahlo exemplify the resilience forged in solitude. Mandela's 27 years of imprisonment provided him with the solitude needed to reflect on his mission and strengthen his resolve. Despite the harsh conditions, he emerged with a renewed sense of purpose and an unbreakable spirit.

Similarly, Frida Kahlo's periods of isolation due to her physical ailments allowed her to channel her pain into her art. Her resilience in the face of adversity became a source of inspiration for countless others. Solitude provided her with the space to process her emotions and transform her vulnerabilities into powerful expressions of strength.

In solitude, we have the opportunity to confront our fears and insecurities. It is a time to reflect on our experiences, learn from them, and develop strategies for moving forward. By embracing solitude during challenging times, we can build the resilience needed to navigate life's ups and downs.

Solitude also allows us to tap into our inner resources. When we are alone, we can focus on our strengths and develop a sense of self-reliance. This self-reliance is a cornerstone of resilience, empowering us to face challenges with confidence and determination.

In conclusion, solitude is a powerful ally in building resilience. By providing a sanctuary for reflection and growth, solitude helps us transform vulnerability into strength and adversity into opportunity. Through the examples of historical figures and our own experiences, we can see how solitude shapes our resilience and empowers us to thrive.

Chapter 4: Solitude vs. Loneliness

There is a clear distinction between solitude and loneliness. While solitude is empowering and self-affirming, loneliness can be debilitating and soul-crushing. In this chapter, we'll navigate the delicate balance between the two, offering insights into how one can transition from loneliness to solitude. We'll discuss the importance of self-compassion, mindfulness, and the ability to enjoy one's own company. Understanding this distinction is key to harnessing the benefits of alone time and preventing feelings of isolation.

Solitude and loneliness are often conflated, but they are fundamentally different experiences. Solitude is a choice, a deliberate embrace of alone time that fosters personal growth and self-discovery. Loneliness, on the other hand, is an emotional state characterized by a lack of connection and a deep sense of isolation.

The transition from loneliness to solitude requires self-compassion and mindfulness. Self-compassion involves being kind to oneself, recognizing that it is okay to seek alone time for self-care and reflection. Mindfulness, the practice of being present in the moment, helps us to appreciate our own company and find peace in solitude.

Developing the ability to enjoy one's own company is essential for transforming loneliness into solitude. This involves cultivating hobbies and interests that bring joy and fulfillment. Whether it's reading, painting, or taking long walks in nature, finding activities that resonate with us can make alone time a source of happiness rather than discomfort.

In solitude, we have the opportunity to connect with our inner selves and discover our true desires and motivations. By embracing solitude with self-compassion and mindfulness, we can prevent feelings of isolation and harness the benefits of alone time.

4

Chapter 5: Finding Beauty in the Mundane

Solitude allows us to see beauty in everyday life. This chapter invites readers to appreciate the small moments and simple pleasures that often go unnoticed. By slowing down and being present, solitude encourages a deeper connection to the environment and a heightened awareness of the world's subtleties. Stories of individuals who have found joy and inspiration in the mundane will illustrate how solitude cultivates an appreciation for the little things, enriching one's life immeasurably.

In the hustle and bustle of daily life, it's easy to overlook the beauty that surrounds us. Solitude provides the space to slow down and appreciate the small moments that often go unnoticed. From the delicate patterns of raindrops on a window to the gentle rustling of leaves in the wind, solitude heightens our awareness of the world's subtleties.

By being present in the moment, we can find joy and inspiration in the mundane. This chapter shares stories of individuals who have discovered the beauty in everyday life through solitude. For example, a gardener who finds peace in tending to plants or a writer who draws inspiration from the quiet moments of reflection.

Solitude encourages us to savor the simple pleasures of life. It allows us to connect with our surroundings in a meaningful way and cultivate an

CHAPTER 5: FINDING BEAUTY IN THE MUNDANE

appreciation for the little things. In this way, solitude enriches our lives and helps us find beauty in the mundane.

5

Chapter 6: The Creative Power of Solitude

Many artists and writers have discovered that solitude is a powerful catalyst for creativity. This chapter delves into the ways in which alone time fosters artistic expression and innovation. We'll explore the practices of renowned creatives who have used solitude to their advantage, from Virginia Woolf to Vincent van Gogh. By understanding the link between solitude and creativity, readers can learn to harness their alone time to unlock their creative potential.

Solitude provides a unique environment for creativity to flourish. When we are alone, we have the freedom to think deeply and explore new ideas without the distractions and judgments of others. This creative freedom is essential for artistic expression and innovation.

Many renowned creatives have used solitude to their advantage. Virginia Woolf, for example, found that alone time was crucial for her writing process. In the quiet of her study, she could immerse herself in her work and let her imagination run wild. Similarly, Vincent van Gogh's periods of solitude allowed him to channel his emotions into his art, creating masterpieces that resonate with people to this day.

In solitude, we can fully engage with our creative pursuits. Whether it's painting, writing, or composing music, alone time provides the space to experiment, take risks, and develop our unique artistic voices. By understanding the link between solitude and creativity, we can learn to

CHAPTER 6: THE CREATIVE POWER OF SOLITUDE

harness our alone time to unlock our creative potential.

6

Chapter 7: Self-Reflection and Personal Growth

S olitude provides a unique opportunity for self-reflection and personal growth. This chapter emphasizes the importance of introspection in understanding oneself and making meaningful life decisions. Through exercises and techniques, readers will be encouraged to engage in self-reflection during their moments of solitude. Personal growth is not a destination but a continuous journey, and solitude is a valuable companion along the way.

Self-reflection is a crucial aspect of personal growth. In solitude, we have the space to look inward and gain a deeper understanding of ourselves. This introspection allows us to identify our strengths, weaknesses, and areas for improvement.

Solitude provides the perfect environment for self-reflection. Without the distractions of the outside world, we can focus on our thoughts and emotions. This chapter offers exercises and techniques to help readers engage in self-reflection during their moments of solitude. For example, journaling can be a powerful tool for exploring one's inner world and gaining clarity on life's challenges.

Personal growth is not a destination but a continuous journey. By embracing solitude and engaging in self-reflection, we can make meaningful

CHAPTER 7: SELF-REFLECTION AND PERSONAL GROWTH

life decisions and cultivate a deeper sense of self-awareness. Solitude becomes a valuable companion on the path to personal growth.

7

Chapter 8: The Strength of Vulnerability

Being alone allows us to confront our vulnerabilities. This chapter examines how solitude can lead to a deeper understanding of one's fears, weaknesses, and insecurities. By embracing vulnerability, individuals can cultivate greater resilience and empathy. We'll share stories of people who have faced their vulnerabilities in solitude and emerged stronger and more compassionate.

Vulnerability is often seen as a weakness, but it is actually a source of strength. In solitude, we have the opportunity to confront our fears, insecurities, and weaknesses head-on. By facing these vulnerabilities, we can gain a deeper understanding of ourselves and develop a sense of self-compassion.

Embracing vulnerability in solitude allows us to cultivate resilience. By acknowledging our weaknesses and working through our fears, we become stronger and more adaptable. This chapter shares stories of individuals who have faced their vulnerabilities in solitude and emerged stronger and more compassionate. For example, a person who has overcome a fear of failure by reflecting on past experiences and learning from them.

In solitude, we can also develop empathy for ourselves and others. By understanding our own vulnerabilities, we can better relate to the struggles of those around us. This empathy enhances our relationships and fosters a sense of connection, even during moments of solitude.

8

Chapter 9: Embracing Solitude in Modern Life

In today's fast-paced world, finding time for solitude can be challenging. This chapter offers practical tips for incorporating alone time into daily life. We'll discuss strategies for setting boundaries, creating a peaceful environment, and prioritizing self-care. Embracing solitude is not about escaping life but about enhancing it, and these tips will help readers integrate solitude into their routines.

The demands of modern life can make it difficult to find time for solitude. However, incorporating alone time into our daily routines is essential for personal growth and well-being. This chapter offers practical tips for embracing solitude in today's fast-paced world.

Setting boundaries is crucial for finding time for solitude. By establishing clear limits on our time and energy, we can create space for self-care and reflection. This might involve setting aside specific times of the day for alone time or saying no to social engagements that do not align with our priorities.

Creating a peaceful environment is also important for enjoying solitude. Whether it's a quiet corner of our home or a serene outdoor space, having a dedicated area for alone time can enhance our experience of solitude. This environment should be free from distractions and conducive to relaxation and reflection.

Prioritizing self-care is another key aspect of embracing solitude. Taking time to engage in activities that nourish our mind, body, and soul can make our alone time more fulfilling. Whether it's practicing mindfulness, reading a book, or engaging in a creative hobby, self-care enhances the benefits of solitude.

9

Chapter 10: The Spiritual Dimensions of Solitude

Solitude has profound spiritual dimensions that can lead to a deeper connection with oneself and the universe. This chapter explores the spiritual benefits of alone time, drawing on insights from various traditions and philosophies. Whether through meditation, prayer, or nature walks, solitude can be a sacred space for spiritual growth and enlightenment.

Solitude provides a unique opportunity for spiritual growth. In the quiet of alone time, we can connect with our inner selves and the universe in a meaningful way. This chapter explores the spiritual dimensions of solitude, drawing on insights from various traditions and philosophies.

Meditation is a powerful practice for experiencing the spiritual benefits of solitude. By quieting the mind and focusing on the present moment, meditation allows us to connect with our inner selves and experience a sense of inner peace. This practice can be done in solitude, providing a sacred space for spiritual growth.

Prayer is another way to experience the spiritual dimensions of solitude. In the quiet of alone time, we can communicate with a higher power and seek guidance and inspiration. Prayer provides a sense of connection and purpose, enhancing our spiritual well-being.

Nature walks are also a powerful way to experience the spiritual benefits of solitude. By immersing ourselves in the natural world, we can feel a deep sense of connection with the universe. The beauty and tranquility of nature can inspire awe and wonder, fostering a sense of spiritual enlightenment.

10

Chapter 11: Solitude and Relationships

Solitude can enhance relationships by fostering self-awareness and emotional intelligence. This chapter examines how alone time can improve one's interactions with others and strengthen bonds. We'll explore the concept of interdependence, where individuals maintain their sense of self while nurturing meaningful connections. Solitude is not a rejection of others but a way to enrich relationships through self-discovery.

Solitude and relationships may seem like opposites, but they are actually deeply connected. Alone time provides the space for self-awareness and emotional intelligence, which are essential for healthy relationships. This chapter explores how solitude can enhance our interactions with others and strengthen our bonds.

Self-awareness is crucial for understanding our needs, desires, and boundaries in relationships. In solitude, we have the opportunity to reflect on our experiences and gain insights into our behavior and emotions. This self-awareness allows us to communicate more effectively and build stronger connections with others.

Emotional intelligence is also enhanced by solitude. By understanding our own emotions, we can better empathize with the feelings of those around us. This empathy fosters deeper connections and improves our ability to navigate conflicts and challenges in relationships.

The concept of interdependence highlights the importance of maintaining a sense of self while nurturing meaningful connections. Solitude is not a rejection of others but a way to enrich relationships through self-discovery. By taking time for ourselves, we can bring our best selves to our relationships and create a more fulfilling and balanced dynamic.

11

Chapter 12: The Transformative Power of Silence

Silence is an integral part of solitude. This chapter delves into the transformative power of silence and its ability to calm the mind and soothe the soul. We'll discuss the benefits of silent retreats, mindfulness practices, and moments of quiet reflection. Silence is a doorway to inner peace and a deeper understanding of oneself.

In a world filled with constant noise and distractions, silence can be a powerful antidote. In solitude, silence allows us to disconnect from the external world and connect with our inner selves. This chapter explores the transformative power of silence and its ability to calm the mind and soothe the soul.

Silent retreats offer a structured environment for experiencing the benefits of silence. By spending time in a quiet, contemplative setting, individuals can achieve a sense of inner peace and clarity. These retreats often incorporate mindfulness practices and meditation, which further enhance the calming effects of silence.

Mindfulness practices, such as meditation and deep breathing, can also be incorporated into everyday life to experience the benefits of silence. By focusing on the present moment and quieting the mind, we can reduce stress and enhance our overall well-being.

Moments of quiet reflection are another way to experience the transformative power of silence. Taking a few minutes each day to sit in silence and reflect on our thoughts and emotions can provide valuable insights and promote self-awareness. Silence is a doorway to inner peace and a deeper understanding of oneself.

12

Chapter 13: Navigating Solitude in Different Life Stages

Solitude can take on different meanings at various life stages. This chapter explores how alone time evolves from childhood to old age. We'll share insights into how solitude can be embraced during pivotal moments in life, from transitioning into adulthood to coping with loss in later years. Each stage of life offers unique opportunities for growth through solitude.

Solitude is a dynamic experience that evolves as we move through different stages of life. This chapter explores how alone time takes on different meanings and forms from childhood to old age, offering unique opportunities for growth and self-discovery.

During childhood, solitude can be a time for imaginative play and exploration. Children often create rich inner worlds during moments of alone time, developing creativity and problem-solving skills. Encouraging solitude in childhood can foster a sense of independence and self-reliance.

As we transition into adulthood, solitude becomes a space for self-reflection and personal growth. In the midst of life's demands and responsibilities, alone time provides an opportunity to reconnect with ourselves and clarify our goals and values. Solitude can help us navigate major life transitions, such as starting a new career or building a family.

In later years, solitude can be a source of comfort and solace. As we cope with loss and changes in our lives, alone time allows us to process our emotions and find a sense of inner peace. Solitude in old age can also be a time for reflection and spiritual growth, as we look back on our life experiences and find meaning in them.

Each stage of life offers unique opportunities for growth through solitude. By embracing alone time at different points in our journey, we can cultivate a deeper understanding of ourselves and live more fulfilling lives.

13

Chapter 14: Solitude as a Source of Innovation

Innovation often springs from solitude. This chapter highlights how alone time can lead to groundbreaking ideas and discoveries. We'll examine the practices of inventors, entrepreneurs, and visionaries who have used solitude to their advantage. By understanding the link between solitude and innovation, readers can learn to harness their alone time for creative breakthroughs.

Solitude provides the perfect environment for innovation to flourish. When we are alone, we have the freedom to think deeply and explore new ideas without the constraints of external influences. This chapter highlights how alone time can lead to groundbreaking ideas and discoveries.

Inventors, entrepreneurs, and visionaries often use solitude to their advantage. For example, Thomas Edison was known for his solitary walks, during which he would brainstorm and develop his inventions. Steve Jobs also valued alone time, using it as an opportunity to think creatively and innovate.

In solitude, we can fully immerse ourselves in our creative pursuits and experiment with new ideas. This unstructured time allows us to take risks and explore unconventional solutions. By understanding the link between solitude and innovation, we can learn to harness our alone time for creative breakthroughs.

Solitude encourages us to think outside the box and challenge the status quo. By removing external distractions and pressures, we can tap into our inner resources and unlock our creative potential. Innovation springs from the freedom and focus that solitude provides.

14

Chapter 15: The Role of Nature in Solitude

Nature provides a serene backdrop for solitude. This chapter explores the therapeutic benefits of spending alone time in natural settings. We'll discuss the calming effects of nature and the ways it can enhance self-reflection and creativity. Stories of individuals who have found solace and inspiration in nature will illustrate the powerful connection between solitude and the natural world.

Nature has a unique ability to enhance the experience of solitude. In natural settings, we can find a sense of peace and tranquility that is often missing from our busy lives. This chapter explores the therapeutic benefits of spending alone time in nature.

The calming effects of nature are well-documented. Research has shown that spending time in natural environments can reduce stress, lower blood pressure, and improve overall well-being. In solitude, nature provides a serene backdrop for self-reflection and relaxation.

The natural world also inspires creativity and innovation. Many artists and writers have drawn inspiration from nature, using it as a source of ideas and imagery. In solitude, we can immerse ourselves in the beauty of the natural world and let our minds wander freely.

Stories of individuals who have found solace and inspiration in nature will illustrate the powerful connection between solitude and the natural world. For example, Henry David Thoreau's time at Walden Pond provided him with profound insights and inspiration for his writing.

Spending alone time in nature allows us to disconnect from the noise of modern life and reconnect with our inner selves. Whether it's hiking through a forest, sitting by a river, or simply enjoying a quiet moment in a garden, nature enhances the experience of solitude and enriches our lives.

15

Chapter 16: Community Support for Solitude

While solitude is a personal experience, community support can enhance its benefits. This chapter examines how communities can create spaces for solitude and encourage individuals to embrace alone time. We'll explore the role of social groups, retreats, and communal practices in fostering a culture that values solitude.

Solitude may seem like an individual pursuit, but community support can greatly enhance its benefits. When communities recognize the value of alone time and create spaces for solitude, individuals can more easily embrace and benefit from it. This chapter examines how community support can foster a culture that values solitude.

Social groups can play a significant role in promoting solitude. For example, book clubs or meditation groups provide structured environments for alone time while also offering opportunities for connection and shared experiences. By participating in these groups, individuals can enjoy the benefits of solitude within a supportive community.

Retreats are another powerful way to experience solitude with community support. Whether it's a silent retreat or a nature retreat, these structured environments allow individuals to immerse themselves in solitude while also benefiting from the guidance and support of facilitators and fellow participants. Retreats provide a safe and nurturing space for self-reflection and personal growth.

Communal practices, such as mindfulness workshops or group art sessions, can also foster a culture that values solitude. These practices encourage individuals to explore their inner worlds and develop a sense of self-awareness, all within a supportive community environment.

16

Chapter 17: Conclusion - The Art of Alone

The final chapter brings together the themes of solitude, curiosity, and resilience to celebrate the art of being alone. We'll reflect on the journey of self-discovery and personal growth that solitude offers. By embracing solitude, readers can unlock their true potential and cultivate a rich, fulfilling life.

In conclusion, solitude is an art that requires practice and mindfulness. Throughout this book, we have explored the themes of solitude, curiosity, and resilience, and how they shape the human spirit. By embracing alone time, individuals can embark on a journey of self-discovery and personal growth.

Solitude is not about being alone; it's about being whole. It is a state of empowerment and self-affirmation, where we can connect with our inner selves and understand our true desires and motivations. Curiosity transforms solitude from a void to be filled into a canvas for exploration and discovery. Resilience is forged in the crucible of solitude, allowing us to thrive despite challenges.

By embracing solitude, readers can unlock their true potential and cultivate a rich, fulfilling life. The art of alone is about finding joy in one's own company and experiencing the world through a curious and resilient spirit.

The Art of Alone: How Solitude, Curiosity, and Resilience Shape the Human Spirit

In "The Art of Alone: How Solitude, Curiosity, and Resilience Shape the Human Spirit," we embark on a transformative journey that reveals the profound benefits of embracing solitude. Through captivating stories and insightful reflections, this book delves into the power of alone time to unlock our true essence, foster creativity, and build emotional resilience.

Explore how solitude, far from being a state of loneliness, becomes a sanctuary for self-discovery and personal growth. Discover the engine of curiosity that drives us to explore the world and our inner selves, turning even the most mundane experiences into opportunities for learning and enrichment. Understand how periods of isolation can fortify our resilience, transforming challenges into stepping stones for success.

From the delicate balance between solitude and loneliness to the serene beauty of nature, each chapter offers practical insights and inspiration for integrating alone time into our busy lives. Uncover the spiritual dimensions of solitude, enhance your relationships through self-awareness, and harness the creative power of silence.

"The Art of Alone" celebrates the unique journey of self-discovery and encourages readers to find joy in their own company. By embracing solitude with curiosity and resilience, we can unlock our true potential and cultivate a rich, fulfilling life.

www.ingramcontent.com/pod-product-compliance
Lightning Source LLC
LaVergne TN
LVHW010442070526
838199LV00066B/6155